The Book of You

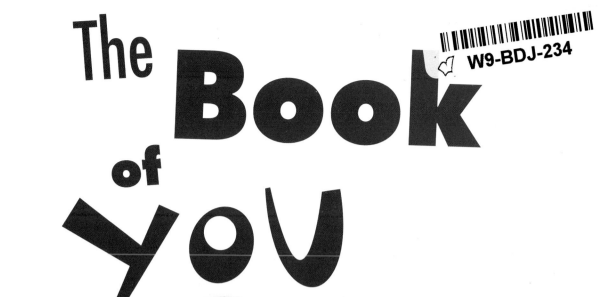

The Science and Fun! of Why You Look, Feel, and Act the Way You Do

Sylvia Funston

Illustrated by Susanna Denti
Photographs by Gilbert Duclos

HarperTrophy
A Division of HarperCollinsPublishers

The Book of You
Text copyright © 2000 by Sylvia Funston
Illustrations copyright © 2000 by Susanna Denti
Photos copyright © 2000 by Gilbert Duclos

First published in Canada by Owl Books/Greey de Pencier Books Inc.,
70 The Esplanade, Suite 400, Toronto, Ontario M5E 1R2
All rights reserved. No part of this book may be reproduced in any manner whatsoever
without written permission except in the case of brief quotations embodied in critical
articles and reviews. Printed in Hong Kong. For information address HarperCollins
Children's Books, a division of HarperCollins Publishers, 1350 Avenue of the Americas,
New York, NY 10019.
Printed in Hong Kong

Library of Congress Cataloging-in-Publication Data

Funston, Sylvia.
The Book of You: the science and fun! of why you look, feel, and act the way you do /
Sylvia Funston ; illustrated by Susanna Denti.
p. cm.
Includes index.
ISBN 0-688-17751-4
1. Psychology—Popular works. I. Title. II. Denti, Susanna, ill.
BF145.F86 2000
150 21—dc21 99-042833

First HarperTrophy edition, 2000

10 9 8 7 6 5 4 3 2 1
Visit us on the world Wide Web!
http://www.harperchildrens.com

Contents

Introduction   4

How You Look   6

Cooking with Genes   8

About Face   10

Handy Things to Know   12

Growing Pains   14

Wannabe   16

What You Do   18

Body Talk   20

Life in a Bubble   22

Lefty or Righty?   24

Brainwriting for Beginners   26

All in the Family   28

The Day You Were Born   30

How You Think and Feel   32

All Kinds of Smarts   34

Come to Your Senses   36

In Your Dreams   38

Don't Forget to Remember   40

Do Boys and Girls Think the Same?   42

What a Personality!   44

This Is Me!   46

Answers   47

Index   48

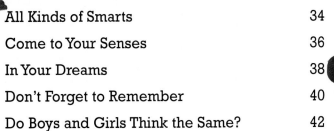

Introduction

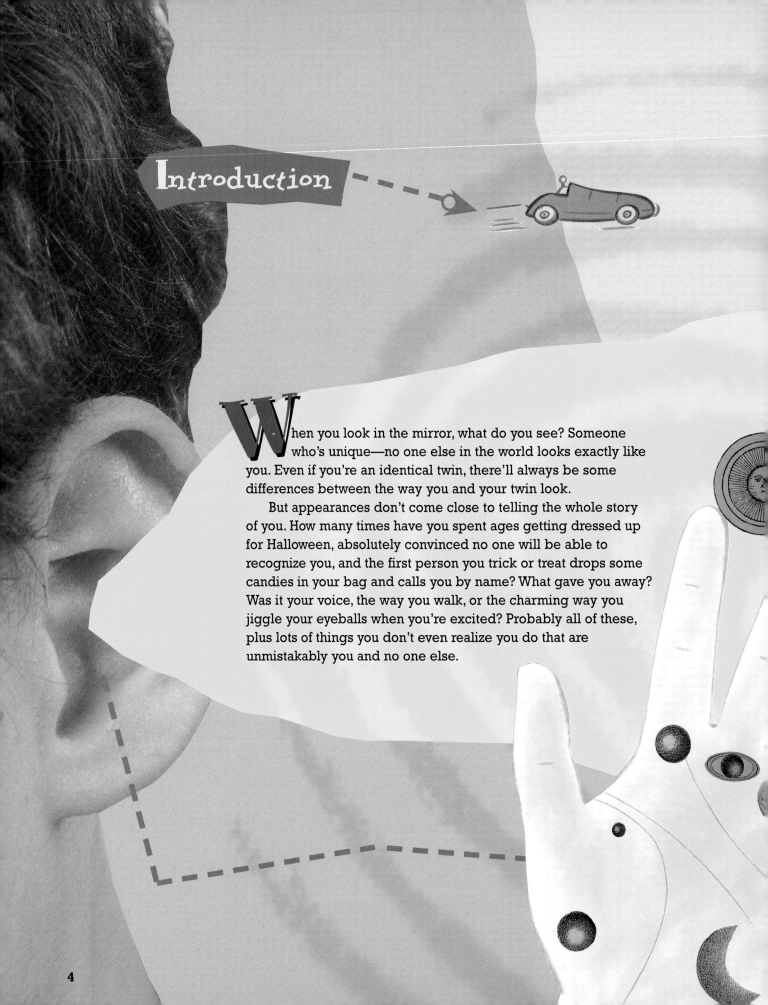

When you look in the mirror, what do you see? Someone who's unique—no one else in the world looks exactly like you. Even if you're an identical twin, there'll always be some differences between the way you and your twin look.

But appearances don't come close to telling the whole story of you. How many times have you spent ages getting dressed up for Halloween, absolutely convinced no one will be able to recognize you, and the first person you trick or treat drops some candies in your bag and calls you by name? What gave you away? Was it your voice, the way you walk, or the charming way you jiggle your eyeballs when you're excited? Probably all of these, plus lots of things you don't even realize you do that are unmistakably you and no one else.

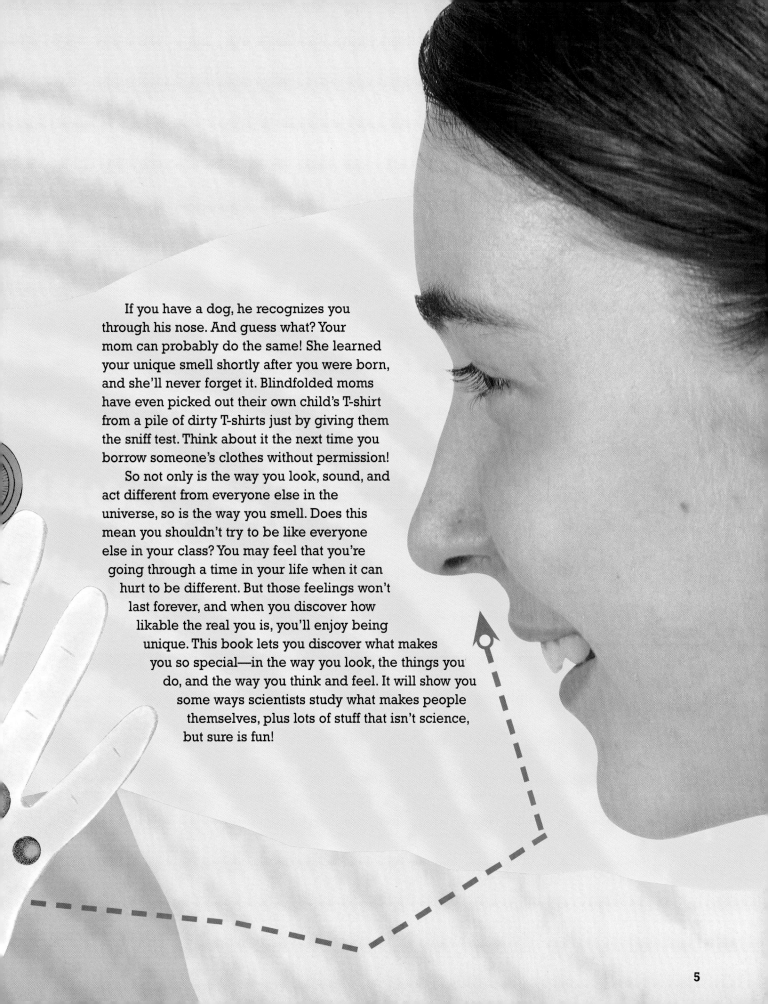

If you have a dog, he recognizes you through his nose. And guess what? Your mom can probably do the same! She learned your unique smell shortly after you were born, and she'll never forget it. Blindfolded moms have even picked out their own child's T-shirt from a pile of dirty T-shirts just by giving them the sniff test. Think about it the next time you borrow someone's clothes without permission!

So not only is the way you look, sound, and act different from everyone else in the universe, so is the way you smell. Does this mean you shouldn't try to be like everyone else in your class? You may feel that you're going through a time in your life when it can hurt to be different. But those feelings won't last forever, and when you discover how likable the real you is, you'll enjoy being unique. This book lets you discover what makes you so special—in the way you look, the things you do, and the way you think and feel. It will show you some ways scientists study what makes people themselves, plus lots of stuff that isn't science, but sure is fun!

⋯⋯⋯⋯⋯⋯⋯⋯⋯⋯⟶

The irises (colored parts) of your eyes have a pattern that is as unique as your fingerprints and can be used to identify you.

How You Look

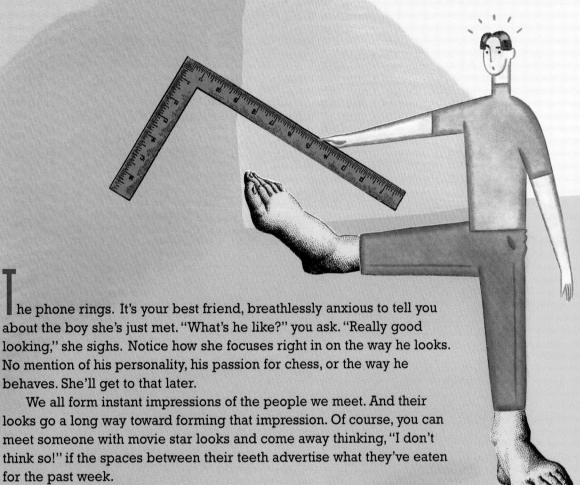

The phone rings. It's your best friend, breathlessly anxious to tell you about the boy she's just met. "What's he like?" you ask. "Really good looking," she sighs. Notice how she focuses right in on the way he looks. No mention of his personality, his passion for chess, or the way he behaves. She'll get to that later.

We all form instant impressions of the people we meet. And their looks go a long way toward forming that impression. Of course, you can meet someone with movie star looks and come away thinking, "I don't think so!" if the spaces between their teeth advertise what they've eaten for the past week.

Looks can be deceiving. The Beast would be the first to agree, with Beauty coming a close second. And they can be confusing. What's considered beautiful in one part of the world might be considered downright ugly elsewhere. Looks can also be fascinating—especially when they're your own.

Those sound like plenty of reasons for starting off this book by taking a close look at how and why you look the way you do.

Only a small percentage of people meet accepted standards of beauty. Imagine how boring life would be if all men looked like heartthrob movie stars and all women looked like supermodels!

Face Fact

Cooking *with* GENES

ecipe for You: Take 23 helpings of deoxyribonucleic (pronounced dee-ox-see-rye-bow-new-clay-ick) acid from Mom and 23 from Dad. Mix together and leave in a warm, dark place to grow for nine months. Hold it right there! What exactly is this tongue-twister of an acid? First of all, everyone calls it DNA. (Guess why.) Who needs it? You—and every other living thing, even dandelions, slugs, and grasshoppers. Each one of the billions of tiny cells that make up your body contains 46 threads of DNA—23 from Dad, and 23 from Mom.

Now You're Cooking!

So where do genes enter into it? Think of your DNA as a cookbook and your genes as its recipes. These gene recipes tell your cells what kind of protein to make. This is important because nose cells, for example, have to do different things than brain cells do, and they need to make different proteins (such as mucus) to be able to do them.

Every single cell in your body contains a DNA cookbook with 50,000 gene recipes. And millions of times every minute your cells use these recipes to cook up new proteins. This is how your body repairs damaged cells, replaces old ones, and grows new ones. And it's how your muscle cells know what shape they're supposed to be and your skin cells know that turning green is out of the question. In fact, your gene recipes tell every cell in your body what it should look like and what it should do.

Each thread of your DNA is made up of two strands that wind around each other, like a twisted ladder. This ladder is built out of four chemicals given the code letters A, T, C, and G. One thread of DNA contains a total of about six billion A's, T's, C's, and G's.

If you could unravel one thread of your DNA, it would be taller than you!

One and Only

If you magnified your DNA threads about 50 million times, you'd see that most of your gene recipes are in the same order as everyone else's. That's because many genes make the same proteins in all human beings. It's where they differ that makes you unique. For instance, the gene recipes for the colored irises in your eyes can belong only to you—just as your vocal cords and the shape of your mouth, teeth, and throat give you a "voice print" that's yours alone.

Mix 'N' Match

Can you match up each protein with the cell that produces it?

Proteins	Cells
❶ I'm red and very attractive to oxygen.	Nose cells
❷ I'm sticky and trap germs and dirt.	White blood cells
❸ I'm slippery and useful for movement.	Red blood cells
❹ I attack invading bacteria and viruses.	Jail cells
❺ I can't wait to get out of here.	Muscle cells

How Old Does Your Nose Feel?

The next time someone asks how old you are, you could truthfully say you don't know. Why? Your DNA is constantly replacing cells. So at any time, parts of you can be as new as they were the day you were born. For instance, the lining of your gut is replaced every three days; your blood cells three times a year; and parts of your skeleton every four years. And, whether you're nine or ninety, the more you learn, the more new brain cells you grow.

About FACE

D oes the face on the opposite page look odd? That's because it's a mish-mash of mismatched features. (Try saying that six times fast!)

We like to look at faces that have a left side that's similar to the right. But nobody's face has two sides that are perfectly matched. Check your own face by holding a mirror down the middle of your school photo. Do you have two different faces when the mirror reflects each side?

Are You Two-Faced?

Scientific study has not proven that your personality is written all over your face. But according to personology, a new way of looking at faces, your right side reflects your dad's traits, and your left, your mom's. If your parents look very different, the two sides of your face should too. (Not that one side grows a mustache while the other has long eyelashes, but in more subtle ways.) Supposedly, the stronger the differences, the greater your mood swings. Does this theory hold true for you?

Personology is based on a set of 68 facial measurements. They were taken of one thousand volunteers' faces. Then the measurements were fed into a computer that matched up facial features with different personality traits. For fun, you can try a personology test yourself on the opposite page.

Your body stops growing some time in your teens, but gravity lengthens your nose and ears throughout your life.

Bumpity-Bump

Personology is one of the latest attempts to find connections between how you look and how you behave. About one hundred years ago, people called phrenologists believed that the bumps on your skull could tell a lot about you. They mistakenly thought your brain was divided into compartments that showed on your skull as bumps. Some compartments were supposed to handle math problems or crossword puzzles, while others took care of personality traits like being pleasant or nosy. The bigger the bump, the more pronounced the ability or behavior. . . . According to this system, if you were really good at math, you'd have a huge bump on your head to prove it!

Personology Test

Find out if your face is trying to tell you anything by picking out your own features on the face below. But before you do, you should know that even personologists feel that how you're brought up and how much you want to alter your behavior can have as big an impact on your personality as, say, the texture of your hair!

The Real You

When you look in the mirror, you see a reverse image of yourself. Check it out. If you have a freckle or a mole on your right cheek, it hops over to the left cheek of your mirror image. To see the real you, you'll need two mirrors, books to prop them up, and face paint or lipstick. Put a mark on the right side of your face. Then angle the mirrors until you can see your entire face in them with the mark on the left. This is how the rest of the world sees you. You look good, don't you? Weird, but good.

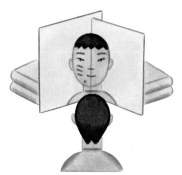

Coarse hair: Your feelings aren't too easily hurt.

An upward sweep to your eyebrows: You're dramatic.

A short distance between eyebrow and eye: You make friends easily.

Eyes that show little white: You express your emotions easily.

Your ears stick out: You like to collect things and might seem to be selfish.

Smooth cheekbones: You're content to stay closer to home.

Fine hair: You might be overly sensitive.

A peak at the top of your eyebrow: You appreciate good design.

A large distance between eyebrow and eye: You hesitate before making commitments.

Eyes that show a lot of white: You make decisions with your head and not your heart.

Laid-back ears: You might waste money.

Prominent cheekbones: You love adventure.

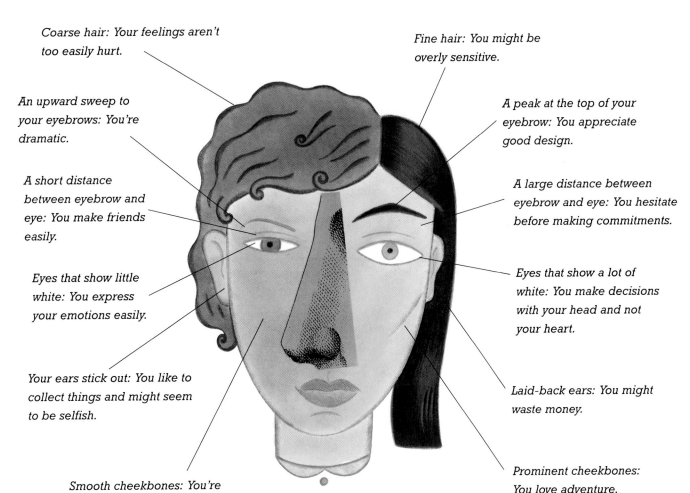

Handy Things to Know

Even if you're not fluent in sign language, personology (see page 10) claims that your hands tell stories about you. Try these and see if you agree.

STORY 1: Hold your hand to the light with your fingers together and palm facing you. If you can see daylight between your fingers, you might be a daydreamer. If not, maybe you're more practical.

STORY 2: Now look at your index finger (next to your thumb) and ring finger (beside your pinkie) on your left hand. If they are the same length, you're supposedly more nimble-fingered than the average kid.

STORY 3: Are you a risk-taker? Check out your ring and index fingers again. If your ring finger is longer, you probably wouldn't say "no" to a dare.

Gotcha!

Reading what personology sees in your hands is just for fun. But science has proven that your hands can definitely tell stories to the police. The skin on your fingers is ridged to give you better grip and traction, and to make you extra sensitive to touch. But these ridges form fingerprint patterns that have been the downfall of many a criminal. To a forensic scientist (who uses scientific evidence to help solve crimes), fingerprints can identify someone and place him or her at the scene of a crime. Even if you're not a criminal, your fingerprint patterns are yours and yours alone.

Fingerprinting

Use a stamp pad to fingerprint like the police do. Make a trial print on spare paper first to mop up excess ink, then slowly roll each fingertip onto paper, from one side to the other. (When you wash your hands after, please don't use the best white towels.)

Collect and identify prints from friends and family and look for similarities and differences. A good fingerprint book from the library can help you learn how to "read" the prints you've collected. For instance, patterns in fingerprints can give clues to where your ancestors came from. While all patterns occur in every nationality, "arches" are very common in people from central Europe; "loops" in people from the rest of Europe; and "whorls" in Australian Aborigines and people from Mongolia.

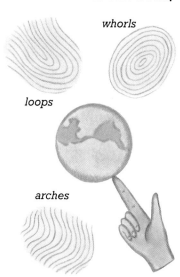

whorls

loops

arches

In the Palm of Your Hand

A palm reader is supposed to be able read the secrets of your present and future life in your hands. Just for fun, look at the hand you use most (it's supposed to contain clues about you as you are today). Compare it with the one on this page. If you are a lefty, look at your left hand and find the same lines there.

Handy Fact

Even identical twins, who share the same gene recipes, can be distinguished by their fingerprints. But one twin might have a fingerprint pattern on the right hand similar to one that the other twin has on the left.

1. **Mound of Mercury** (ability to think quickly)
   Large, plus pointed fingers: good public speaker
   Has short, straight lines: good doctor or nurse
   Hollow and unlined: likely to be shy

2. **Mound of Apollo** (artistic ability, enthusiasm)
   Large: extravagant
   Medium: pleasant, sunny nature
   Close to Mercury: success in the arts

3. **Mound of Saturn** (caution, love of solitude)
   Large: serious-minded
   Leans toward Apollo: appreciate beauty
   Close to Jupiter: aim high

4. **Mound of Jupiter** (pride, ambition, and leadership)
   Large: ambitious
   Medium: self-confident
   Small: dislike authority

5. **Upper mound of Mars** (persistence, ability to endure)
   Large: watch your temper
   Medium: courage
   Flat: easily afraid

6. **Mound of the Moon** (imagination)
   Large: imaginative
   Medium: sensitive, romantic, artistic
   Flat: unsympathetic

7. **Lower mound of Mars** (personal drive)
   Large: a risk taker
   Medium: can get things moving
   Small vertical lines: discreet

8. **Mound of Venus** (capacity for love)
   Large: loads of energy
   Medium: warmhearted and compassionate
   Small: bit of a loner

9. **Heart line** (emotions)
   Steeply curved: warmhearted
   Close to fingers: head rules heart
   Many small branches: like meeting people

10. **Head line** (intelligence, concentration, and memory)
    Steeply sloped: intuitive and imaginative
    Straight across palm: highly intelligent
    Head and life line begin separately: independent mind

11. **Life line** (health and vitality)
    Long, well marked: happy, healthy life
    Reaches outer edge of hand: lots of travel

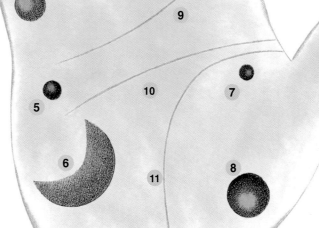

Growing Pains

Since before you were born, you've been growing steadily. By the time you're ten, your head and brain are almost fully grown. Soon (if it hasn't already happened) you'll notice that your hands and feet seem too big for your body. Then your arms and legs will seem to go on forever. Your torso (the part between your waist and neck) will eventually get the message and lengthen to catch up with the rest.

Everyone goes through these three stages of growth, and they do it at their own speed. Some kids grow in spurts, adding 10 cm (4 in.) or more to their height in a year. Others just seem to slowly lengthen until one day their feet reach the end of the bed. (You do a lot of growing in bed. So your parents aren't just trying to wreck your social life when they nag you about bedtime.)

Look Up!

If you're a girl whose cells are following gene recipes for growth spurts, you'll probably start sprouting two years before most boys. (Now you know why girls can be a pain in the neck to boys!) But, soon it will be the girls' turn to get a neck cramp. Boys usually keep growing long after most girls stop.

While your gene recipes play an important role, what you eat also helps decide how tall you'll grow. Healthy food will do a lot more for your bones and height than fast food.

How Tall Will You Grow?

Here's a way of estimating how tall you'll be. Take your current height, find out on the chart what percentage it is of your full adult height, then do some quick x and ÷. (This method is only an estimate. If you discover you're going to be tall enough to guarantee yourself a future with the NBA, double-check your math.) And remember, there is no such thing as a correct height. Whatever height you end up when you've finished growing will be exactly right for you.

$$\frac{\text{Present height (cm or inches)}}{\text{\% of full adult height (see chart)}} \times 100 = \text{your adult height}$$

Here's an example based on an 11-year-old girl who is 148 cm (58 in.) tall:

$$\frac{148}{88.4} \times 100 = \frac{14800}{88.4}$$

14800 ÷ 88.4 = 167 cm (66 in.)

Your Age	Percentage of your full adult height	
	Boys	Girls
8	72 %	77.5 %
9	75 %	80.7 %
10	78 %	84.4 %
11	81.1 %	88.4 %
12	84.2 %	92.9 %
13	87.3 %	96.5 %
14	91.5 %	98.3 %
15	96.1 %	99.1 %
16	98.3 %	99.6 %
17	99.3 %	100 %
18	99.8 %	100 %
19	100 %	100 %

You're a Giant, Relatively Speaking

One of the oldest known ancestors of human beings, *Afarensis*, lived about 3 million years ago. An adult *Afarensis* wasn't very tall and would have barely met the height requirements for the scarier theme park rides today. Human beings have done some growing over time, and we're still at it! You're taller than your great-grandparents were at your age. Why? It's your comfortable lifestyle and plenty of healthy food.

Measuring Up

Most people share the same body proportions. Do these average measurements work for you? Because you're still growing, chances are they might not—yet. Look on page 47 to see a magazine survey of how other kids measured up.

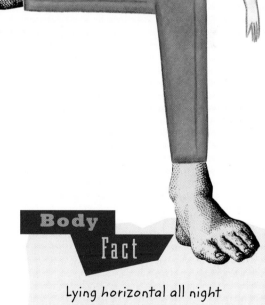

Height = **Width**

Your height equals the distance between your outstretched fingertips.

Forearm = Foot

The length of your foot equals the distance between your wrist and elbow.

Height = Head length x 7 (approximately)

As a one-year-old, your body was four times longer than your head (from crown to chin). When you're fully grown, it could be up to eight times.

Fist **= Foot**

Here's one that the magazine readers weren't asked about: The distance around your closed fist equals the length of your foot.

Body Fact

Lying horizontal all night cancels out the squash-effect that gravity has on your spine, so you're taller before breakfast than at any other time of the day.

Wannabe

or at least five thousand years, people around the world have pinched, pulled, tugged, starved, stuffed, scarred, tattooed, or bound their bodies to try on one idea of what's beautiful after another. Coneheads, flat foreheads, behinds that stick out, flat behinds, flat chests, big chests, muscle-bound legs, thin legs, tiny waists, big bellies, and pumped-up muscles all came and went as fashion dictated.

Today, the tall, slender runway model look is all the rage. For most of us this is an impossible goal. Even models, who owe their "perfect" looks to make-up artists, hair stylists, and photographers, don't often live up to their glossy magazine images when they are just walking down the street. And if they can't live up to expectations, what chance do the rest of us have?

You've Got It

Everyone wishes at some time that they looked like someone else. While you can't change your gene recipes, you can make the most of what your genes gave you. You can look terrific whether your basic body shape is short and naturally rounded, medium-sized and muscular, tall and thin, or a combination of these shapes. The secret to looking good is to give your body the healthy food it needs, plus lots of water, and plenty of exercise. A well-toned body with healthy, glowing skin looks great in any size or shape.

Where would you find a drowned chicken, a sleeping dog, and a chest of drawers? On the heads of European women two hundred years ago.

They were all elaborate hairstyles that took so long to create, women wore them for weeks. This meant they had to sleep upright with wooden supports under their chins, duck or enter doorways on their hands and knees, and poke their hairdos out of special trapdoors in the tops of their sedan chairs.

Trust Yourself

Part of feeling good about your body is being sure of its abilities. Even if you don't have the lightning-fast reflexes, balance, and agility of a world-class athlete, you can improve your natural abilities and boost your confidence.

Speed Up Your Reactions

How fast you react depends on your ability to see something, decide what to do, and then do it. Try the ruler drop to test your reaction times. Test yourself several times a week and watch your reactions speed up.

❶ Hold out your hand with your thumb and index finger in an open pincer grip (like a crab claw).

❷ Ask a friend to hold a 30 cm (12 in.) ruler upright 2.5 cm (1 in.) above the space between your thumb and finger.

❸ Without telling you when, your friend should drop the ruler. You have to catch it between your thumb and finger.

❹ The shorter the distance the ruler falls, the faster your reaction time. (Most people catch the ruler after it's fallen between 15 and 20 cm [6 to 8 in.].)

Zap!

Every second, 12 billion nerve cells carry 1,000 electric signals around your body at an average speed of about 130 m (400 ft.) per second. That's a fact. But it's also thought that the color pigments in your eyes just might affect the speed of nerve messages to your brain. The darker your eyes, the faster the zap! If you have dark eyes, chances are you're good at sports like baseball, which require fast hand-eye coordination. If you have lighter colored eyes, you have a better chance of excelling at sports like golf, in which players can choose their own timing.

Write Fact

When you write the word "the" (it doesn't apply to printing), do you join up the t and h at the base then go back to cross them? If you do, then a fun look at graphology says you're an enthusiastic, responsible person who doesn't mind following rules.

What You Do

You've found out why you look the way you do. Now it's time to look at some of the things you do.

Start with something you can easily observe. When you're with your best friend, for instance, do you find yourself copying his or her body movements? Do you both tilt your head in the same direction or stand on one foot when you're listening to someone else talk? The closer your friendship, the more you copy each other's movements.

Once you've clued into this secret, you can tell at a glance who's really friendly and who's not. While you're looking for copycat clues among your friends, look for distance clues too. Without even thinking about it, people stand closest to those they love and trust. If someone says they really like you but never gets within arm's length of you, something's wrong. Either they're not telling the truth, or you're putting way too much garlic on your breakfast cereal.

Researchers have had fun trying to figure out why we act the way we do. What if, some of them ask, our DNA contains recipes for more than just the way we look? What if it also contains recipes for the way we behave?

If you had to enter a room full of strangers and walk across an empty space to greet someone, you'd instinctively cross one arm across your body to set up a barrier between you and the room. Notice how many famous people do the same—although they look as if they're fixing their shirt cuffs, watch straps, bracelets, or purses.

Body Talk
Fact

Body TALK

Without doing it, think about clasping your hands with your fingers interlocked. Quick—which thumb sits on top? Most people have to do it to give the right answer. So go ahead. Now try again so the opposite thumb is on top. Does it feel weird?

The way you clasp your hands is just one of hundreds of actions that make up your body language. These gestures are so much a part of you, you don't realize you're doing them. But while all humans use the same kind of body talk, your gestures and expressions are as personal as your fingerprints. No matter if you're crossing your arms, smiling, brushing your teeth, waving good-bye, or tying your shoelaces, you nearly always perform the same movements in the same way every time.

Smile Please

You're born instinctively knowing some of your body talk, but you have to learn the rest. Which gestures are inborn? Take smiling as an example. When you smiled for the first time your parents were thrilled. Did you learn by copying the smile on your parents' faces? The answer lies with blind babies. They can't see what their parents do, but babies blind from birth smile just like other babies do. That means the human smile is built in, not learned.

Foreign Bodies

Many North American and British people use the same hand gestures. But if they traveled in southern Europe, their body talk might be misunderstood. For instance, making a circle sign with your index finger and thumb to signal that something is okay (like in the photo on page 32) might get you into trouble in the south of France. There it means something is worthless! And be careful directing traffic in southern Europe. If you tried to beckon someone toward you with a palm-up wave, you'd be telling them to back up!

Give-Away Laughter

Your smile is unique, and so is the way you laugh. Some people think your laugh gives away secrets about you. Which description best fits the way you laugh? Turn to page 47 to see what that might say about you.

❶ Giggle (nervous little laugh)
❷ Cackle (loud, piercing laugh)
❸ Snort (laugh bottled up until it bursts out)
❹ Snigger (quiet, under-the-breath kind of laugh)
❺ Guffaw (just like Santa)

Smile Fact

How good are your fake smiles? There are 18 different types of smiles, but just one is real. It's known as the Duchenne smile and it uses two sets of muscles— one around the mouth, which you can move deliberately, and another around the eyes, which responds only to genuine emotion. Your eyes will crinkle only when your smile's for real.

WHAT, Me Lie?

Even if you don't want it to, your body language leaks information about what you're thinking and feeling. That's why it's easier to lie with words than with your body. Answer true or false to the following questions to find out how good you are recognizing when someone is lying. Check your answers on page 47.

I think people might be telling lies when:

❶ They can't look me in the eye.
❷ They move their arms around a lot.
❸ They hold their hands in front of them, palms up, fingers slightly curled.
❹ They absentmindedly rub or scratch their face or twirl their hair.
❺ They sit or stand in a relaxed way with little movement.
❻ They raise their inner eyebrows.
❼ They blush.
❽ They don't blink very much.

Life in a BUBBLE

Y ou're in a crowded elevator. What do you do? If you're like most people, you face the door. Then, with a blank look on your face, you study the flashing floor numbers as if they hold the secret of life. What is it about you and your fellow passengers that makes you act so weird?

Here are some clues. Everyone has it, even babies. As you grow, it grows. It takes up more space in front of you than behind. And it shrinks when you're with people you trust. Got it yet? It's your personal space. Think of it as an invisible force field with you at its center.

Too Close for Comfort

Most people don't intrude into other people's space bubbles unless invited. But sometimes, like in crowded elevators or on rush-hour trains and buses, we're forced to be uncomfortably close. Then we shrink our space bubbles, and avoid feeling threatened by pretending other people don't exist. We don't make eye contact or let our faces show that we know they're there.

Your space bubble gives you a small territory over which you're boss. By learning how and when to give up some of your rights, you cooperate with others and defuse stressful situations without having to use your fists!

Bubble Fact

People who live or work together often include favored objects in their personal space. For instance, does your home have a "Dad" or a "Mom" chair that no one else sits in? And do you all have your own places around the table?

How Big Is Your Space Bubble?

You'll need:
- some friends
- a tape measure
- pencil and paper

❶ Ask a friend to stand 2 m (7 ft.) away from you. (Measure toes to toes.)

❷ Have your friend look only at your chin and, with arms by his or her side and no facial expression, walk slowly toward you. Look at your friend's eyes.

❸ Say "stop" the moment you feel your friend is too close.

❹ Measure and record your space bubble distance, toes to toes.

❺ Repeat with other friends.

❻ Add up all the space bubbles and divide by the number of friends to find your average space bubble distance with friends.

❼ Repeat the experiment with your best friend and your family. Is there a difference in the results?

Space at Your Fingertips

You can also use your arm to check the size of your space bubble. Next time you're talking to someone you know, and you're comfortable with the distance between you, raise your arm. Is the space between you the full length of your arm (shoulder to fingertips), from shoulder to wrist, or shoulder to elbow? If you're a fingertip-length person, you'd feel at home in North America and Western Europe. Eastern Europeans stand closer (shoulder to wrist). And people from Mediterranean and Middle Eastern countries think you're standoffish if you're farther away than elbow distance.

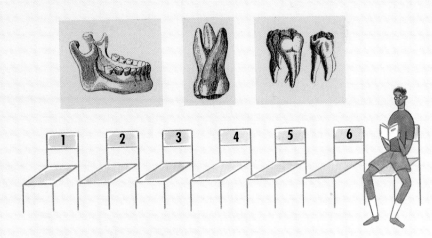

Take a **Seat**

Imagine you're going to the dentist. When you walk into the waiting room it looks like this. Which chair would you probably sit on? Another person comes in after you. Which chair do you think they'd choose? Now turn to page 47 to see if you make the same seat choices as most people would.

Lefty or RiGHTY?

If you were asked to trace around one of your hands, which one would you choose? About 90 percent would use their right hand to trace around their left. Humans have favored the right for a long time. More than 80 percent of hand tracings left on cave walls by Cro-Magnon people were of the left hand, showing that even then (about 14,000 years ago) most people were right-handed.

The Right Stuff

Why are most humans right-handed? People used to believe it had to do with soldiers carrying their shields on their left arms to protect their hearts. But why were there so many righties before shields were invented—and why were so many nonfighting types also right-handed? Today we know it has something to do with the brain. The brain is organized so that the left side controls everything on our right, and vice versa. But no one fully understands how it all works and why in every group of one hundred people, at least seven or eight of them will be left-handed.

Eye Spy

Just as you prefer using one hand over the other, so you have a preference for one of your eyes. To find out which one it is, point at an object across the room. Without moving your finger, close one eye. If your finger lines up with the object, the eye you're looking through is your dominant eye. If it doesn't, look through the other eye. (If it still doesn't line up, go get your eyes checked!)

Scrambled Brains

Which side of your brain do you use to speak and read? Scientists have shown that most righties and 70 percent of lefties use the left side of the brain. Of the remaining lefties, half (about 15 percent) use the right side, and the rest (another 15 percent) use both sides. Some researchers say the way you hold your pen provides a clue to how your brain is organized. Which picture fits the way you write? Check page 47 to find out what it says about how your brain might be organized.

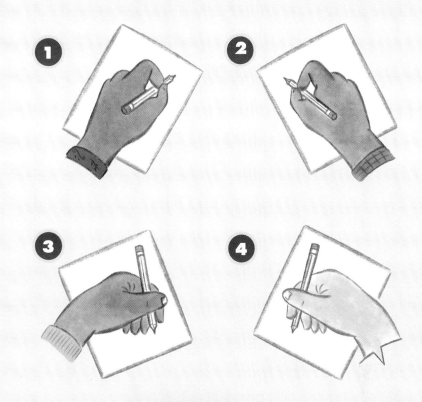

Handy Fact

If you have two left-handed parents, you have a slightly greater chance of being a lefty than a righty. Also, boys have a slightly greater chance than girls.

How Right OR LEFT ARE YOU?

It's unusual to be ambidextrous—able to use both hands equally well. It's equally rare to be unidextrous—using only one hand. The majority of people use different hands to do different things, making them mixed-handed. What about you? Do you use your right hand or your left hand (or both) to do these tasks?

Writing	Brushing your teeth
Washing your hair	Opening a drawer
Throwing a ball	Unscrewing a jar lid
Holding a racket	Operating a mouse
Opening a door	(not the kind that squeaks)
Cutting with scissors	Operating a joystick

Brainwriting for BEGINNERS

How many sheets of paper have you used practicing your signature? Everyone does it. Your signature is a sign of who you are, so you want it to say good things about you. But can people really tell things about you from your handwriting?

The study of handwriting is known as graphology. You've probably seen crime shows where the expert witness helps to crack the case by examining a writing sample. That's one kind of graphology, in which experts use handwriting to identify the writer.

You Are What You Write

The other, less scientific kind of graphologist claims that handwriting reveals secrets about your personality. As you grow older, your handwriting changes and you develop your own style. Even if your writing style is still developing, though, it probably contains enough hints of your grown-up style to make it fun to analyze. (But this is just for fun. Most graphologists will only analyze adult handwriting.)

Write On

To get a good sample of your writing, copy the sentences below onto a sheet of white, unlined paper. Write at your normal speed and size and forget about being super neat. No ruled lines please—this is not a school test. Then look at the page opposite to see what you can discover. (Try this test again next year to see how your handwriting has changed.)

Jigs had short, stubby legs, one on each corner of his square, bulldog body, and a squished-in nose. One ear flopped forward, the other looked as if it could if it wanted to but couldn't be bothered. When Jigs was nervous both ears stuck out sideways like two fat helicopter blades ready to whisk him away at the first sign of trouble. The trouble was, it usually came in the shape of Arthur, boss cat of the neighborhood.

What **Handwriting** Might Reveal About You

What to look for	What it means
Size	
Large writing	Outgoing and enthusiastic
Small writing	Able to accomplish goals
Slant of letters	
Upright slant	Reliable and mature
Leftward slant	Eager to please
Rightward slant	Affectionate and sociable
Direction of lines	
Lines rise toward the right	Optimistic and ambitious
Lines dip toward the right	Need to look more on the bright side (or you might be tired)
Lines dip at the very end	Don't like planning ahead
Lines rise up in the middle	You need to be challenged or you become bored
Lines dip down in the middle	Hard worker
i-dots	
Weak dot	Work on your self-confidence
No dot	Good at making decisions
Circle dot	Trying to look cool
Capital letters	
Too large	Like attention
Too small	Sympathetic to other people's needs
Narrow	A careful nature
Narrow and tall	Sensitive and emotional
Wide	Self-reliant and imaginative

Write Fact

Some people think handwriting should be called brainwriting because it reflects our inner thoughts and feelings.

All in the FAMiLy

Honest
Outgoing
Aggressive
INDEPENDENT
Timid
Optimistic
Tactful
Generous
Mean
Secretive
Intelligent
Kind
Tender
Practical
Curious
Self-centered
Impractical
Loud
Gentle
Jealous
Ambitious
Patient
Confident
iMPATiENT
Pessimistic
Bossy
Creative
Shy
Adventurous
Caring
Arrogant

Which of the words to the left best describe you? Were you born with these personality traits, or did they develop as you did? In other words, is your personality shaped by your gene recipes or your upbringing? Scientists are trying to decode our DNA, and studying how our upbringing affects us—they call it the "nature versus nurture" debate. But we still don't know all the answers. For now, people look for clues where they can find them.

One place to start is with identical twins who were separated at birth and raised by different families. Identical twins carry the same gene recipes, so if genes affect how we behave, identical twins should do similar things regardless of how they are raised. When one set of separated identical twins finally met, they discovered that they both tap the table when they're talking and snap their fingers when they can't come up with an answer. Other identical twins learned they both sneeze loudly in a crowd as a joke and also share the habit of keeping rubber bands on their wrists, dipping buttered toast in their coffee, and flushing the toilet before using it. Genes or coincidence?

Your Order, Please

Scientists who think that your upbringing has a huge influence on how you act look for clues in the way families interact. One question they're trying to answer is whether your birth order (whether you were born first, second, third, etc.) affects how well you cope with life. They've discovered that some birth order spots seem to create extra stress, while others might help people develop a wider variety of interests, take on more responsibility or feel that no one listens to them. Some psychiatrists even suggest you should consider birth order when deciding whom to marry.

A Twin-Fest

Every year, tens of thousands of twins travel to Twinsburg, Ohio, to take part in the annual twin festival. If you peek inside the carnival tents at the festival, instead of palm readers you'll find scientific researchers. Identical twins are crucial to the "nature versus nurture" research. So researchers love to make contact with new sets of twins to help with their projects. And what better opportunity than at the greatest twin-fest on earth?

Family Fact

First-borns often feel they have to achieve more than younger brothers or sisters. Of the first 23 American astronauts sent into space, 21 of them were born first or were only children.

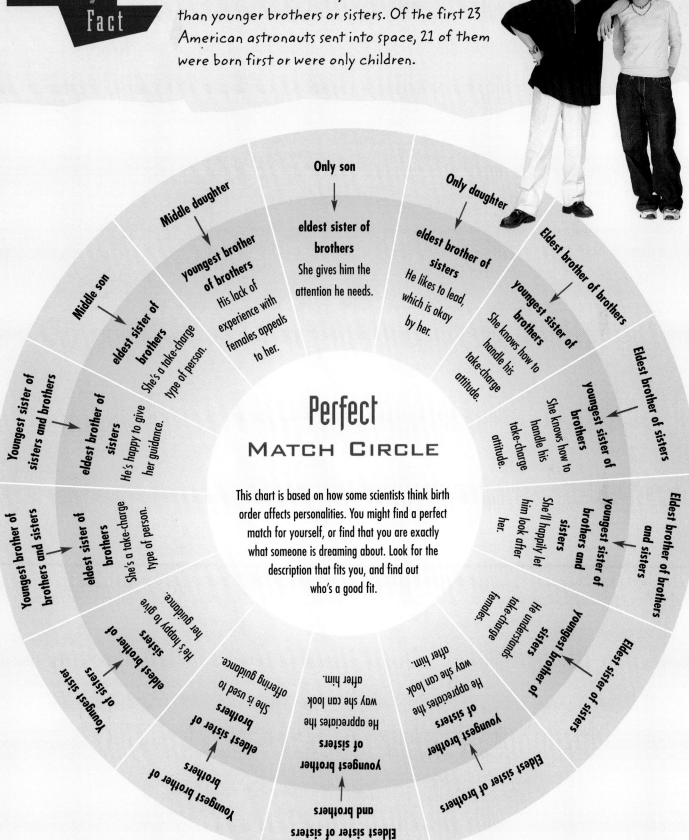

Perfect
MATCH CIRCLE

This chart is based on how some scientists think birth order affects personalities. You might find a perfect match for yourself, or find that you are exactly what someone is dreaming about. Look for the description that fits you, and find out who's a good fit.

Only son → **eldest sister of brothers** She gives him the attention he needs.

Only daughter → **eldest brother of sisters** He likes to lead, which is okay by her.

Middle daughter → **youngest brother of brothers** His lack of experience with females appeals to her.

Middle son → **eldest sister of brothers** She's a take-charge type of person.

Youngest sister of sisters and brothers → **eldest brother of sisters** He's happy to give her guidance.

Youngest brother of brothers and sisters → **eldest sister of brothers** She's a take-charge type of person.

Eldest brother of brothers → **youngest sister of brothers** She knows how to handle his take-charge attitude.

Eldest brother of sisters → **youngest sister of brothers** She knows how to handle his take-charge attitude.

Eldest brother of brothers and sisters → **youngest sister of brothers and sisters** She'll happily let him look after her.

Eldest sister of sisters → **youngest brother of sisters** He understands the take-charge females.

Eldest sister of brothers → **youngest brother of sisters** He appreciates the way she can look after him.

Eldest sister of sisters and brothers → **youngest brother of sisters** He appreciates the way she can look after him.

Youngest brother of brothers → **eldest sister of brothers** She is used to offering guidance.

Youngest sister of sisters → **eldest brother of sisters** He's happy to give her guidance.

Youngest brother of sisters → **eldest sister of brothers** She is used to offering guidance.

Eldest sister of sisters and brothers → **youngest brother of sisters** He appreciates the way she can look after him.

29

The Day You Were Born

Your gene recipes and your upbringing might work together to decide how you act, but it's going to take a lot more research to know for sure. Meanwhile, many people like to believe that when you were born also influences your personality and the things you do. Thousands of years ago, people realized that twelve patterns of stars appear to circle around the sky each year. Ancient astrologers related these star patterns (or constellations) to the twelve monthly signs of the zodiac (from a Greek word meaning "little animals"). People believed then, and many still do, that the position of the planets, sun, and moon in these star patterns at the time of someone's birth influences the way they approach life.

What's Your Sign?

Most people know their sun sign, the constellation that the sun was in when they were born. Each sun sign in the zodiac covers about thirty days in the calendar. Astrologers claim that people born under the same sign have the same general characteristics. Check out the Star Chart to see if the descriptions seem to match what you know about yourself, your family, and friends. What do you think? Could there be something to it?

Number Fact

Numerology can let you have fun with your full name. Use this chart to convert the letters into numbers. The sum is your name number. (See how to, right.) Check your result on page 47.

1	2	3	4	5	6	7	8	0
A	B	C	D	E	F	G	H	I
J	K	L	M	N	O	P	Q	R
S	T	U	V	W	X	Y	Z	

What's Your Number?

Numerology is the study of numbers to try to figure out what makes you tick. Say you were born on April 12, 1992. To find your birthdate number, convert your birthdate into numbers, which would be 04/12/1992. Then add these numbers together until you end up with a single digit, like this:

$0 + 4 + 1 + 2 + 1 + 9 + 9 + 2 = 28$

$2 + 8 = 10$

$1 + 0 = 1$

So far, so good. But what does having 1 as a birthdate number say about you? Look on page 47 to see what a numerologist might say.

From Beginning to End

Some astrologers believe that people born at the start of a sign can be quite different from those born at the middle or end. Each sign lasts about a month. If your birthday is in the first part, read the first line under your sign's date, the second if it's in the middle, and the third if it's in the last part. And if you're born on the cusp—the few days where one sign ends and the other begins—read the last line of the earlier sign as well as the first line of the later one.

Aries the Ram

March 21 to April 20
- Single-minded, courageous, honest.
- Determined, energetic, organized.
- Lighthearted, charming, curious.

Taurus the Bull

April 21 to May 21
- Kind, loyal, stubborn, artistic.
- Organized, logical, good at math.
- Serious, responsible, loyal.

Gemini the Twins

May 22 to June 21
- Intelligent, persuasive, funny.
- Charming, artistic, good with words.
- Creative, likes change and excitement.

Cancer the Crab

June 22 to July 23
- Sensitive, artistic, practical.
- Secretive, imaginative, loyal.
- Tolerant, curious, compassionate.

Leo the Lion

July 24 to August 23
- Proud, practical, determined.
- Wise, funny, good listener.
- Energetic, stubborn, enjoys change.

Virgo the Virgin

August 24 to September 23
- Logical, warmhearted, organized.
- Disciplined, stubborn, charming.
- Hardworking, motivated, perfectionist.

Libra the Balance

September 23 to October 23
- Artistic, imaginative, romantic.
- Serious, fair-minded, creative.
- Logical, gifted with words, sociable.

Scorpio the Scorpion

October 24 to November 22
- Ambitious, competitive, magnetic.
- Creative, imaginative, enjoys excitement.
- Sensitive, caring, puts people first.

Sagittarius the Archer

November 23 to December 21
- Intelligent, energetic, likes travel.
- Spontaneous, risk-taker, enthusiastic.
- Creative, courageous, warmhearted.

Capricorn the Goat

December 22 to January 20
- Serious, hardworking, devoted friend.
- Sociable, energetic, kind.
- Intelligent, creative, full of ideas.

Aquarius the Water Carrier

January 21 to February 19
- Intelligent, curious, sociable.
- Optimistic, determined, idea person.
- Sensitive, charming, offbeat sense of humor.

Pisces the Fish

February 20 to March 20
- Romantic, creative, uses heart not head.
- Considerate, caring, imaginative.
- Flexible, able to cope well with change.

················►

Some foods, such as chocolate, alter your mood by triggering the release of feel-good chemicals in your brain. No wonder most people like chocolate so much!

How You Think and Feel

Do you play a musical instrument? Is it a pain to have to practice? Here's a fact that might take some of the pain away. People who learn to play musical instruments as children develop more connections in their brains than people who don't. If you want to have *really* scary brainpower, take up the violin.

Even if you can't play a note, your brain's abilities still make the most sophisticated computer look about as smart as a rock. Yes, that thing inside your head is one of the wonders of the world. It keeps you informed about what's going on around you, makes regular checks on what your body's up to, works overtime while you sleep, and does all kinds of things without you even being aware of it. It's also the source of your emotions. Without them, you wouldn't make it as a human being—nor would you be able to reason properly.

No one really knows how much of your intelligence is inherited from your parents, and how much you pick up from the way your family treats you as a child and the way your life develops. Like many other things about you, however, your brain develops in a unique way and, like your body, benefits from regular exercise.

Your eyes give away your thoughts and emotions. When you look at someone or something you really like, the pupils of your eyes open wide.

Feelings Fact

All Kinds of SMARTS

Your brain looks like a giant walnut made out of pinkish gray jelly. If you could pull it out of your head and set it on the table, it wouldn't look very impressive. Yet that floppy brain is one of the most complicated objects in the universe.

Your brain makes billions of connections, making you the most intelligent known creature in the Solar System. But scientists have trouble agreeing on exactly what intelligence is. There seem to be different types of intelligence. Being good with numbers and words is one kind. Musical ability, artistic ability, being able to understand and get along with other people, and being able to understand yourself are others.

No one can claim top marks in every kind of intelligence. Albert Einstein was a genius at math and abstract thinking, and could probably read a map standing on his head, but he wasn't great at understanding himself or other people.

What's the Q?

IQ is short for intelligence quotient. Remember "quotient" from math? It's what you get when you divide one number by another. Your IQ is determined by dividing your mental age from a standard test result by your real age, then multiplying by 100.

People used to think IQ tests told the whole story about intelligence, but they were wrong. Having emotional intelligence, or EQ, can help you succeed in almost every career you can think of. And if you're planning to become a designer, an architect, or an artist, you'll also need spatial intelligence, or SQ. Discover something about yours on the next page.

How's Your EQ?

Unlike your IQ, your EQ continues to improve as you mature. But what is it? If you have high EQ you are:

1 self-aware (you know your own strengths and weaknesses)
2 able to control your emotions
3 self-motivated (you try to improve, and can wait for a reward)
4 good at reading other people's feelings
5 good at handling relationships

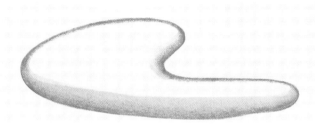

Brain Fact

There's long been a belief that fish is "brain food." Now scientists know why. Your brain needs a particular type of unsaturated fat—omega 3—which is found in fish.

How's Your SQ?

The great artist Pablo Picasso had terrific spatial intelligence, though he was lousy at schoolwork. This meant he could look at a plan of a house and imagine what it would look like when it was built. How's your spatial intelligence, or SQ? To find out, count the blocks in this shape, then check your answer on page 47. Take your time and think about it.

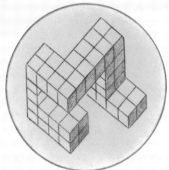

Boost YOUR EQ

Here's a good way to prepare yourself emotionally so you don't lose your cool.

❶ Make a list of things you enjoy and keep it with you.

❷ When you feel negative emotions getting the better of you, stop what you're doing. Breathe in slowly while you count five, then breathe out slowly to a count of five. Repeat until you feel more in control.

❸ Ask yourself, "Do I want to feel like this?" If the answer is yes, then continue to feel that way, but try not to take your feelings out on other people. (After all, it was *your* choice.)

❹ If the answer is no, pull out your list and pick an item. If, for example it's walking along a beach, imagine the feel of warm sand beneath your feet, and the sounds of waves and seagulls.

❺ Ask yourself how you'd rather be feeling or acting. Imagine you're feeling or acting that way now.

❻ Take three or four deep breaths to bring your attention back to your body and focus on the present.

Come to Your SENSES

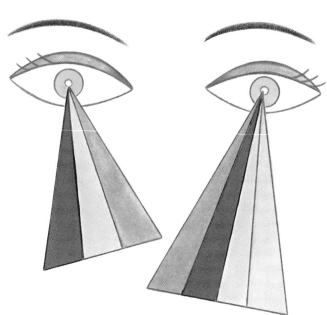

Every second, you do something amazing. You sense the world around you. Your eyes see millions of shades of color; your nose smells the difference between toothpaste and morning breath; your tongue tastes the difference between bananas and broccoli; your skin senses the lightest touch and the smallest change in temperature; and your ears not only hear a pin drop but also tell you whether you're going around in circles.

A Sixth Sense?

Some researchers believe we have something called "blindsight." They asked some blind people to tell them which side of a television screen contained a cross. They couldn't, because they couldn't see the screen. Then the researchers asked the same blind people to *guess* which side the cross was on. Their answers were almost as good as those of a sighted person who could see the screen! The results might mean that information from the blind peoples' eyes was being processed, but they just weren't conscious of it.

Sending Senses

After collecting all that information, your five senses send it to your brain. How your brain gathers it together so you're aware of your surroundings is still a mystery, and a miraculous one at that. For instance, when you look at your face in the mirror, its image is collected by a flat layer of cells at the back of your eyeball. So your brain's first impression is flat like a photo. Thousands of bits of information from this flat image are sent to the vision center at the back of your head. There, some groups of cells see color, while others see shape, lines, angles, edges, movement, and so on. Somehow your vision center puts this jigsaw of information together instantly to form a three-dimensional image of your face.

WHAT'S YOUR Dominant Sense?

Senses
Fact

Want to know how to read your friends' minds? All you have to do is memorize seven eye movements that will tell you how they're thinking, and whether their dominant sense is sight, hearing, or touch. Next time you're studying with friends, ask a question and watch what their eyes do while they think of the answer. Then look at the chart below to see what it means. (Note that these eye clues work for most right-handed people, and left or right means from the point of view of the person asking the questions.)

Eye Movements	What's happening in the brain	Dominant Sense
Up, to the right	Searching memory for visual images	Sight
Up, to the left	Creating new images	Sight
Straight, to the right	Searching memory for sounds or words	Hearing
Straight, to the left	Creating new sounds or words	Hearing
Down, to the right	Listening to "inner voice"	Hearing
Down, to the left	Accessing touch (also smell or taste) feelings	Touch
Stare straight ahead	Accessing visual information	Sight

Your skin is the largest organ in your body. It contains 3,500,000 sense receptors (200,000 of them sense cold, 500,000 sense touch and pressure, and 2,800,000 sense pain).

Make Sense of Your Senses

Do you rely most on what you can see, hear, or touch? Here are other clues you can use to discover your dominant sense. One is the way you describe your thoughts. For example, if you're a vision person, you might say, "I see what you mean." If you're a hearing person, you might say, "I hear what you're saying." If you rely more heavily on touch, you might say, "I feel that's true!" Or try to remember something like a friend's phone number. How do you bring it to mind? Do you visualize the buttons you push? Do you remember the tones the numbers make when you dial? Or do you remember what it felt like to press the buttons in a particular pattern?

In Your DREAMS

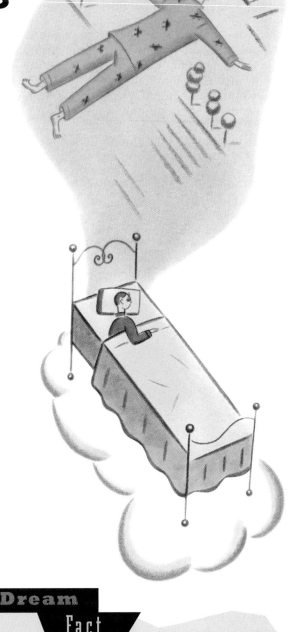

As you drift off to sleep at night, the electrical waves created by your brain slow down. Eventually you enter what is known as slow-wave deep sleep. After about ninety minutes, parts of your brain suddenly become even more active than when you're awake. But you're not—you're dreaming. You've entered REM sleep, named after the rapid eye movements beneath your closed lids. It's during this kind of sleep that you do your most vivid dreaming. Your first REM dream lasts only about ten minutes, but REM dreams keep occurring every ninety minutes, with each dream lasting longer than the one before.

Why Do You Dream?

No one knows for sure. One idea is that your dreaming brain works to solve problems for you. It explores your memory for possible solutions and uses them to create dream after dream, throughout the night. If you feel less worried when you wake, it might be because of dream problem-solving. Maybe that's why, if you have a problem, you're told to sleep on it.

What if You Don't Dream?

Volunteers took part in experiments in which they were woken up each time their brains started to slip into REM sleep. They reported starting to dream when they were awake, suddenly seeing things that weren't there. When these volunteers were finally allowed to sleep without interruption, their brains took large amounts of REM sleep to make up for what they had missed. Obviously, we need our REM sleep. Some scientists believe we sleep partly to be able to dream.

Dream Fact

The front part of your brain, which is the thinking, logical part, stays fast asleep while you're dreaming.
Do you suppose that's why dreams are so crazy?

scnacedelihskr

Can you unscramble these letters to form the name of a famous author? In a dream experiment, only the letters were presented to a woman. She thought about the anagram as she drifted off to sleep, then jotted down her dream when she awoke. First she dreamed about an actress with a hairstyle like her friend Carol's. The next night she dreamed about a cairn terrier that wanted to be carried. She was struck by the fact that the letters "ca" kept cropping up, so she thought again about the word Carol. Eventually it brought to mind Christmas. When she put Christmas and Carol together she got Christmas Carol. Have you solved the puzzle yet? (Check your answer on page 47.)

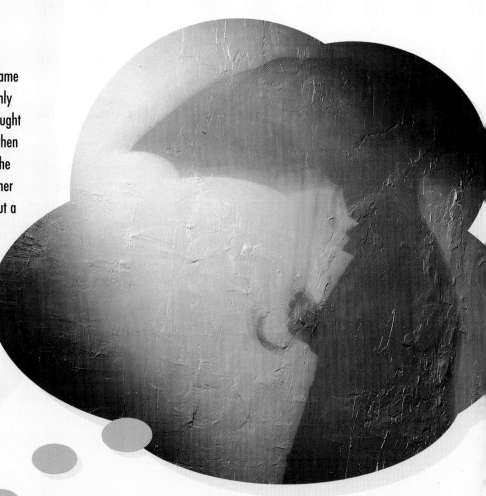

How to Change Your Dreams

Sometimes, when you're worried, you experience the same upsetting dream over and over again. In other words, you have a recurring nightmare. Researchers think this might happen when your dreaming brain can't solve a problem and so can't create a new dream. Your nightmare is your brain's call for help. But how can you help when you're sound asleep? Say in your nightmare you're being chased by a shadowy figure you can't identify. You can help your sleeping brain by finding out about the shadow. The next time you drift off to sleep, tell yourself to turn around in your dream and face the shadow so you can see who it is. (Remember, nothing can hurt you in your dreams.) You might be surprised at the results. Facing up to fears in your dreams may help you conquer them in your waking life.

Don't Forget to
REMEMBER

Your memory is something else that's unique about you, but how it works is a mystery. One part of the brain stores memories, and another pulls out information when you need it, like for a test at school (well, some of the time). But your memories are scattered all over your brain. Imagine your favorite ice cream. Can you see it, smell it, taste it, and feel how cold it is? You can do all that in your imagination because, in a flash, memories are pulled from your vision center (at the back of your head), your smell and taste center (right behind your nose), and your touch center (running like a hairband across the top of your head). Your brain somehow links them together and . . . voilà, chocolate mint ice cream with extra chocolate chips.

Memory 1-2-3

You have three types of memory. The first is your working memory. Without it, you'd forget every word in this sentence as soon as you read it, so you couldn't link the words together to make sense out of them. The second is your short-term memory. It lasts between thirty seconds and a few hours. This one prevents you having to wander around looking for where you left the book you were reading before you went out to the movies. The third is your long-term memory, the type you need for tests. Researchers think that if you repeat something often enough, a short-term memory becomes permanent and is stored as a long-term memory. It's like saving something to the hard drive on your computer.

KIM'S Game

In Rudyard Kipling's novel *Kim,* the orphan Kim O'Hara is trained as a secret agent. Here's a traditional version of the game Kim played to sharpen his observational memory. Take two minutes to study all the objects in the picture. Then close the book and list as many objects as you can recall. (Take this game to the next level for your friends. Make up questions they have to answer about the objects. For example, "How many dots are on the dice?" or "Does the teapot have a lid?")

Memory Fact

Researchers think the best way to remember random information is to turn it into a story because our brains are very good at taking in and remembering stories.

Memory Tricks

You can boost your memory power with a few memorizing tricks. Try making up a silly sentence using the first letters of words you want to remember. For instance, "King Philip climbed over fifty gentle spacemen" can help you remember that plants and animals are classified by Kingdom, Phylum, Class, Order, Family, Genus, and Species. You can also look for rhymes or acronyms. For example, the acronym HOMES will make sure you never forget that Huron, Ontario, Michigan, Erie, and Superior are the names of the Great Lakes.

Do Boys and Girls THiNK the Same?

Girls and boys look different, and sometimes act like they come from different planets. But are they different where it counts the most—inside their heads? Do boys have an edge in understanding machines, maps, and math? Are girls better at communicating, quickly recognizing patterns and colors, and doing intricate finger work and certain memory tasks? The trouble with ideas like these is that there are always exceptions.

Every human brain is made up of two halves, joined by a thick band of nerve fibers that passes messages between them. The band in a girl's brain is thicker in some parts than in a boy's brain, so it might be able to handle messages faster. Researchers use a scanning machine to see people's brains at work and to check out the connections. When girls solve a word puzzle, they spread the work over both halves. Boys seem to build stronger connections within each half of their brains, so only one half gets involved in solving a word puzzle. It seems girls' brains are better networked, and boys can focus their attention more closely. One writer compared the way brains work to different types of lights—if most girls have floodlights for brains, most boys have spotlights.

What About Your Brain?

Like everything else about you, your brain is unique. If you're a girl who's good at jigsaws, map reading, math, and fixing things, or if you're a boy who's good at communicating, solving word puzzles, or quickly spotting hidden patterns, don't worry—you're not a freak! Lots of things—gene recipes from your parents, hormones from your mother before you were born, opportunities and encouragement while you were growing up—combined to make your brain what it is today.

BOY Puzzles, GIRL Puzzles

Try these puzzles, then find out which tests researchers think you should find easier on page 47. But remember, it's what you achieve that counts, not what you're *supposed* to achieve.

Letter sounds
In your mind, how fast can you run through the alphabet and count all the letters, including the letter E, that contain the sound "ee"?

Letter shapes
Run quickly through the alphabet in your mind again, but this time count the number of capital letters that contain curves.

Identical shapes?
Are these block shapes identical? To find out you have to turn them in your mind.

Word power
Grab a piece of paper and copy out the letter pairs below. You have one minute to add two letters (back or front) to each of these pairs of letters to form a four-letter word.

MA   SP   NE   WH   SI   OG   DU   FO

How Many Brains Do You Need?

Your brain is really four brains in one. At the bottom, what's called your reptilian brain takes care of things like breathing and sneezing. Wrapped around it at the back of your head, your cerebellum coordinates messages between your muscles, balance organs, and thinking brain, so you can ride a bike without having to think about every move. Perched on top of your reptilian brain is your feeling brain, which plays a big role in your emotions and memory. And sitting on top of everything is your thinking brain. Some research shows that boys use the more primitive part of their feeling brain to handle their emotions while girls use the more recently developed part. Is this why some boys are more likely to use their fists to show anger, while many girls prefer to use words?

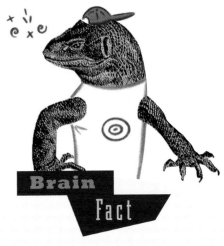

Brain Fact

Men have slightly larger brains than women, because they are larger overall. But they don't have more brain cells. Women just package theirs in a slightly smaller space.

What a  PERSONALITY!

You can be attractive, great at sports, and a genius at school, but the thing that leaves the most lasting impression is your personality. So take a few minutes to figure out the basic characteristics that make you who you are. If everyone's personality is made up of several characteristics, the ones we prefer become strongest and determine our "type." To help discover what those preferences are, researchers have identified eight basic personality characteristics and matched them up in pairs.

Pair 1: Extroversion and Introversion

This pair measures whether you prefer spending time with other people, or having quiet times alone.

Pair 2: Sensing and Intuition

These show whether you are more daydreamy or practical in the way you take in information about the world around you.

Pair 3: Thinking and Feeling

These show whether you tend to make decisions with your heart or with your head.

Pair 4: Judging and Perceiving

This pair measures whether you prefer an organized, or a flexible, way of life.

What are your preferences?

To find out, grab a piece of paper and do the quiz on the next page. Remember that what makes you unique can't possibly be captured in a quiz in a book like this. Just have some fun with it and don't take your findings too seriously!

What Do You Really Think of You?

A lot of people think that you need high self-esteem to be successful. But the truth is, you can have real doubts about yourself and still achieve great things. (Ask any famous person.) If your answers to these questions reveal that your opinion of yourself could do with some TLC, ask an adult you trust to talk to you about how you feel. (To find out how to score your answers, see page 47.)

Choose one for each statement below

Strongly Agree   Agree   Disagree   Strongly Disagree

1 On the whole, I am satisfied with myself.

2 At times I think I am no good at all.

3 I feel that I have a number of good qualities.

4 I am able to do things as well as most other people my age.

5 I feel I do not have much to be proud of.

6 I feel useless at times.

7 I feel that I am a person of worth, at least the equal of others.

8 I wish I could have more respect for myself.

9 All in all, I am inclined to feel that I am a failure.

10 I take a positive attitude toward myself.

PERSONAL PREFERENCES QUIZ

Do you Strongly Agree/Agree/Disagree/or Strongly Disagree with these statements?

❶ Extroversion and Introversion

a. I like to be around people and can be lonely without them.

b. I enjoy being with people some of the time, but need time to be alone to read and think.

c. I'm outspoken and make friends easily.

d. I find it hard to speak out and I make friends slowly.

e. I tend to be impulsive and think about things after I've done them.

f. I like to think things through before doing them.

g. I find it easy to talk about myself.

h. I find it difficult to talk about myself.

❷ Sensing and Intuition

a. I follow instructions and notice details.

b. I ignore instructions and tend not to notice details.

c. I'm realistic, practical, and sensible.

d. I'm imaginative and think a lot.

e. I like to do things the way they're usually done.

f. I like to make up new ways of doing things.

g. I'm a very down-to-earth person.

h. I'm often described as having my head in the clouds.

❸ Thinking and Feeling

a. I use my head to make decisions.

b. I'm likely to make decisions from the heart.

c. In solving problems I always try to see things from a logical point of view.

d. In solving problems I always put people's needs first.

e. I usually take a firm stand on most issues.

f. I can be persuaded by personal needs on most issues.

g. I think people who make decisions from the heart are illogical.

h. I think people who make decisions only with their heads are cold and inhuman.

❹ Judging and Perceiving

a. I prefer to get things settled and know where I stand.

b. I like to go with the flow.

c. I like to make deadlines and stick to them.

d. Deadlines are only reminders of what needs doing—they can be changed.

e. I work hard and always prepare for jobs and clear up afterwards.

f. I work hard when I'm in the mood and hate preparing for jobs or clearing up afterwards.

g. I like to get on with things and hate wasting time.

h. I'm quite happy to wait and see what happens.

Done? Now check your choices on page 47 to find out the four characteristics that form the basis of your personality. What do you think of this assessment of your personality? Complete baloney, or a glimpse at what makes you tick?

This Is ME!

Now you get to really have some fun. Sit down at a computer, or grab some paper and pens, and design a wall chart where you can record all of your newfound knowledge about yourself in one place. Below are some examples of the kind of information you might like to include. Add anything else you can think of, and include a current photo of yourself with the date marked on it. If you do a new one around the same time each year, it will be a great way to keep a record of what changes (and what stays the same) about you as you get older.

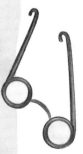

- Name
- Signature
- Age
- Height and predicted height
- Weight
- Shoe Size
- Hair color
- Hair texture (fine, medium, or coarse)
- Hair type (curly, wavy, or straight)
- Color of eyes
- Shape of face (round, oval, or square)
- Fingerprint type (loops, whorls, or arches)
- Basic body shape (rounded, muscular, or thin)
- Size of personal space (fingertip, wrist, or elbow distance)
- I'm a righty/lefty

- I look most like/sound most like/laugh like (name family members)
- I have the same hair/eyes/nose/lips/ears/chin, etc. as (which family members?)
- Birth order in the family
- Birthdate
- Astrological sign
- Birthdate number
- Name number
- Earliest memory
- Best subjects at school
- Favorite hobbies
- Favorite book/TV show/kind of music
- Dominant sense
- Characteristic gesture
- Personality type
- The word my friends or family would use to describe me

Answers

Page 9   Mix 'n' Match
1 – red blood cells; 2 – nose cells; 3 – muscle cells; 4 – white blood cells; 5 – jail cells

Page 15   Measuring Up
Height = Width. This was true for 50% of the magazine readers surveyed. The rest said they were shorter. **Forearm = Foot.** For 68% of readers surveyed, this measurement was true. **Height = Head length x 7.** For 40% of readers surveyed, their head length was 6 to 6.5 times their height; 40% said it was 7 to 7.5 times.

Page 21   Give-Away Laughter
1. You're fun-loving and always look on the bright side. 2. You're confident and like to meet people. 3. You're thoughtful and maybe a little shy. 4. You're relaxed and easygoing. 5. You're happiest when you're the center of attention

Page 21   What, Me Lie?
1. **False.** In some cultures, it's rude to look people in the eye. Also, some experienced liars force themselves to look directly at the person to whom they're lying so that they will appear as if they have nothing to hide. 2. **False.** A liar is afraid of "non-verbal leakage" in which his body language tells the true story while his words tell the lie, so to reduce the possibility of leakage he keeps his hands as still as possible. Some people even go so far as to sit on their hands. 3. **True.** This is known as a hand shrug and is a sign that the person speaking is trying to disown his or her words. 4. **True.** The hand starts out moving toward the mouth to hide the lie, then carries on to another part of the face. Someone scratching or rubbing a pretend itch to hide a lie does it in a very halfhearted way. 5. **False.** It's difficult not to squirm when you're telling lies because you'd like to escape from the situation but the need to tell a lie keeps you rooted to the spot. Experienced liars learn not to squirm, but they still find it difficult to control small body movements. 6. **True.** You have to watch very carefully for this involuntary raising of the inner eyebrows because it happens very fast. 7. **True.** Some of the time, because not everyone blushes when they're embarrassed. 8. **False.** Blinking is usually a sign that the brain is working overtime—in this case trying to come up with plausible excuses.

Page 23   Take a Seat
Most people entering the waiting room would sit in seat 3. The next person to enter would usually select seat 5.

Page 25   Scrambled Brains
If the researchers who think pen-holding style is important in determining how your brain is organized are right: 1. The right side of your brain controls your speech. 2. The left side of your brain controls your speech. 3. The left side of your brain controls your speech. 4. The right side of your brain controls your speech.

Page 30   Number Fact and What's Your Number?
If your number is: 1. You're a natural leader and determined to succeed. 2. You're a good team player and can inspire others. 3. You're full of enthusiasm and can make others feel good. 4. You're steady and reliable and make a faithful friend. 5. You're popular and can adapt quickly to change. 6. You're creative, responsible, and a fair judge of situations. 7. You work well on your own and often come up with new ideas. 8. You're an organized achiever who enjoys helping others. 9. You're a creative leader who cares about other's feelings.

Page 35   How's Your SQ?
There are 56 blocks in the shape. If you got the answer right, you have good SQ. If not, you can improve your SQ through practice. Getting to know how to use maps is a good way. Learning how to draw is another.

Page 39   scnacedelihskr
A Christmas Carol is one of author Charles Dickens's best-loved novels. And "Charles Dickens" is the solution to the anagram.

Page 43   Boy Puzzles, Girl Puzzles
Letter Sounds: There are 9 "ee" sounds in the alphabet. They are: B, C, D, E, G, P, T, V, and Z. **Letter Shapes:** There are 11 capital letters with curves in the alphabet (B, C, D, G, J, O, P, Q, R, S, U). **Identical Shapes?** Yes, the shapes are identical. **Word Power:** Some possible words are: made, maid, make, mane, maps; spar, spat, spit, spry, gasp, rasp, wasp; news, newt, bone, cane, cone, gone; what, when, whip; side, sire, site, silo, sing; clog, smog, ogle, ogre; duck, dull, dumb; foam, fond, fort, foul. Research shows that girls generally do better on puzzles like Letter Sounds and Word Power. Boys generally do better on activities like Letter Shapes and Identical Shapes? Do your results tally with these research findings? Don't be surprised if they don't. Many girls ace tests that are supposed to be easier for boys, and vice versa. We're all unique and full of surprises.

Page 44   What Do You Really Think of You?
For questions 1, 3, 4, 7, and 10, give yourself 4 points every time you chose Strongly Agree; 3 points for each Agree; 2 points for each Disagree; and 1 point for each Strongly Disagree. For questions 2, 5, 6, 8, and 9, give yourself 1 point every time you chose Strongly Agree; 2 points for each Agree; 3 points for each Disagree; and 4 points for each Strongly Disagree. Most people score between 30 and 40. A smaller number of people score between 30 and 20. If you score below 20, talk to your parents or your teacher about how you feel.

Page 45   Personal Preferences Quiz
Give yourself 4 points each time you chose Strongly Agree; 3 points for each Agree; 2 points for each Disagree; and 1 point for each Strongly Disagree.
If you score between 9 and 16 points on questions 1a, c, e, and g, you're an extrovert.
If you score between 9 and 16 points on questions 1b, d, f, and h, you're an introvert.
If you score between 9 and 16 points on questions 2a, c, e, and g, you're a senser.
If you score between 9 and 16 points on questions 2b, d, f, and h, you're intuitive.
If you score between 9 and 16 points on questions 3a, c, e, and g, you're a thinker.
If you score between 9 and 16 points on questions 3b, d, f, and h, you're a feeler.
If you score between 9 and 16 points on questions 4a, c, e, and g, you're a judger.
If you score between 9 and 16 points on questions 4b, d, f, and h, you're a perceiver.

What does this mean? Here's what your characteristics say about you:
Extroversion = Outgoing;
Introversion = Reserved;
Sensing = Literal-minded;
Intuition = Creative;
Thinking = Logical;
Feeling = People-oriented;
Judging = Organized;
Perceiving = Flexible

Index

Afarensis, 15
Ambidextrousness, 25
Anger, 43
Artistic ability, 34, 35
Astrology, 30–31

Beauty, 7, 16
Birthdate, 30, 31
Birth order, 28, 29
Blindness, 20, 36
Blinking, 21, 47
Blushing, 21, 47
Body:
  growth stages of, 14, 15
  healthy, 16
  image, 16
  largest organ in, 37
  proportions, measuring, 15
  shape/size, 16
Body language:
  and dominant sense, 37
  and lying, 21, 47
Boosting:
  EQ (emotional
    intelligence), tips, 35
  memory, tips, 41
Boys:
  brains of, 42, 43
  growth rate of, 14
  and handedness, 25
  puzzles, 43, 47
Brain:
  of boys, 42, 43
  cells, 8, 43
  and dreaming, 38, 39
  and eye movements, chart,
    37
  food for, 35
  fully grown, 14
  functions of, 33
  of girls, 42, 43
  how organized, 24, 25, 42,
    43
  and intelligence, 33, 34
  left side of, 24, 25, 47
  and memory, 40, 43
  nerve messages to, 17
  parts of, 43
  right side of, 24, 25, 47
  and senses, 36

Cells, 8, 9
Cerebellum, 43
Cheekbones, and
  personality, 11
Cold, sensing, 37
Compatibility, and birth
  order, 29
Constellations, 30
Copying (behavior), 19
Crimes, solving:
  and fingerprinting, 12
  and handwriting, 26
Cro-Magnon people, 24
Cultural differences:
  beauty, ideas of, 7
  body language, 20
  fingerprints, 12
  lying, 47
  personal space, 23

Deoxyribonucleic acid.
  See DNA
DNA, 8–9, 28
Dominant sense, tests, 37
Dreams, dreaming:
  how to change, 39
  why you dream, 38
Duchenne smile, 21

Ears, 11, 36
Einstein, Albert, 34
Emotions:
  boosting control of, tips, 35
  and brain, 43
  and intelligence, 34, 35
  and palm reading, 13
  source of, 33
EQ (emotional intelligence):
  boosting, 35
  what it is, 34
Estimating tallness, chart, 14
Exercise, 16
Eyebrows, 11, 21, 47
Eye contact, 21, 47
Eyes:
  color of 6, 9
  color and nerve messages,
    17
  dominance, test, 24
  and emotions, 11, 33
  irises, 6, 9
  reactions, chart, 37
  and smiling, 21

Face, 10–11
Fashion, 16
Fears, and dreaming, 39
Feeling brain, 43
Fingerprints, 9, 12, 13
First impressions, 7
Fish (brain food), 35
Food, healthy, 14, 15, 16, 35
Friendliness, judging, 19

Games:
  memory, improving, 41
  proteins/cells, matching, 9
Gender differences:
  brain, 42, 43
  growth, 14
Gene recipes, 8–9
Girls:
  brains of, 42, 43
  growth rate of, 14
  puzzles, 43, 47
Graphology (study of
  handwriting), 18, 26–27
Growth stages, 14

Hair, 11, 17
Hand-eye coordination, 17
Hands:
  handedness, 24, 25
  and lying, 21, 47
  and personality, 12–13
Handwriting, 18, 26–27
Hearing, 36, 37
Height, 14–15

Identical twins, 4, 13, 28
Intelligence, 33, 34–35
IQ (intelligence quotient), 34
Iris (eye), 6, 9

Laughter, 21, 47
Left-handedness, 24, 25, 37
Left side:
  of brain, 24, 47
  of face, 10
  and fingerprints, 13
Long-term memory, 40
Lying, recognizing, 21, 47

Magazine images, 16
Measuring:
  personal space, 23
  proportions of body, 15
Memory:
  boosting, tips, 41
  and brain, 40, 43
  types of, 40
Mirror image, 11
Mixed-handedness, 24, 25
Models, 7, 16
Molecules, 8
Musical ability, 33, 34

Nature versus nurture, 28
Nerve cells, 17
Nightmares, 39
Numerology, 30, 47

Omega 3 (fatty acids), 35

Palm reading, 13
"Perfect" looks, 16
Perfect Match Circle, 29
Personality:
  and astrological sign,
    30–31
  and birthdate number, 30,
    47
  and birth order, 28, 29
  and facial features, 10, 11
  and fingers, 12–13
  and handwriting analysis,
    26, 27
  and name number, 30, 47
  and palm reading, 13
  type, 44–45, 47
  and upbringing, 28
Personology, 10, 11, 12
Phrenology, 10
Problem-solving, during
  dreams, 38, 39
Proteins, 8
Puzzles:
  anagram, 39, 47
  girls, boys, 43, 47

Reactions, speeding up
  (exercise), 17
REM (rapid eye movement)
  sleep, 38
Reptilian brain, 43
Right-handedness, 24, 25, 37
Right side:
  of brain, 24, 47
  of face, 10
  and fingerprints, 13

Self-control, boosting, 35
Self-doubts, 44
Self-esteem, 44
Sense receptors, 37
Senses:
  dominant, 37
  and memory, 40
  sending, 36
  sixth, 36
Short-term memory, 40
Signs, astrological, 31
Sixth sense, 36
Size:
  of body, 16
  of brain, boys/girls, 43
  of DNA, 9
Skin, 12, 36, 37
Skull, bumps on, 10
Sleep, 15, 38
Smell, 5, 36, 40
Smiling, 20, 21
Space, personal, 19, 22–23
Sports, ability in, 17
SQ (spatial intelligence),
  34, 35
Star Chart, 31
Star patterns
  (constellations), 30

Tallness, estimating, 14
Taste, 36, 40
Tests, quizzes:
  dominant eye, 24
  EQ (emotional
    intelligence), 34
  handwriting analysis, 26,
    27
  lying (recognizing), 21, 47
  personology, 11
  personal preferences,
    45, 47
  reaction time, 17
  self-esteem, 44, 47
  SQ (spatial intelligence),
    35, 47
Thinking brain, 43
Touch, 36, 37, 40
Twins festival, 28
  (See also Identical twins)

Unique self:
  and appearance, 4
  and body language, 20
  and genes, 9
  keeping a record of, 46
  personal preferences quiz,
    44, 45
  and senses, 5
Upbringing, 11, 28, 33

Vision, 36, 37, 40

Working memory, 40

Zodiac, 30